THE TAO OF THE JEDI

THE TAO TE CHING
MEETS STAR WARS

Based on Lao Tzu's **Tao Te Ching**
and inspired by George Lucas' **Star Wars**

Translation and commentary by
Oliver Benjamin

The Ministry of Jediism | www.ism.co/jediism

Published by:
The Ministry of Jediism / Dudeism LLC
www.ism.co/jediism

Homepage for this book: www.ism.co/library/jediism

A long time ago, in a principality far, far away...

In China around 500 BC, the *Tao Te Ching* was written by Lao Tzu. It was a deep philosophical look at life, the universe and everything. Today it ranks as one of the most widely translated books on Earth, second only to the Christian Bible.

About 2477 years later, *Star Wars* was written by George Lucas. It was also a deep, philosophical look at life, the universe and everything. It is one of the most celebrated movies in history.

What many people don't know is that Star Wars was deeply influenced by the *Tao Te Ching*.

By incorporating elements from Star Wars in this new adaptation of the *Tao Te Ching*, we can easily see how elegantly these two classics intersect.

May the Force (and the Tao) be with you!

CONTENTS

PREFACE

For many westerners, George Lucas' Star Wars was their first real exposure to eastern philosophy, although they might not have known it at the time. In fashioning the Jedi philosophy, Lucas drew on several different religious traditions, however the central metaphysical concept in the film, *the Force* was based upon the Chinese notions of Tao and Chi, its light and dark sides mirrored in the concept of yin and yang.

The concept of Tao has been enshrined most notably in the Chinese religion which derives its name from it: Taoism. One of the oldest continually-practiced religions in the world, Taoism has undergone many changes over its 2500 years and even merged with other religions (Zen Buddhism is a mixture of Taoism and Buddhism). Because of its passive and undogmatic nature, it has been overtaken in popularity by other religions and is not very well-known today, outside of China at least.

Tao is normally translated as "way" in English, an ordering principle to the universe that also describes the manner in which it unfolds. On a human level, to be in accordance with Tao means that you are working in harmony with nature and deriving strength from its momentum and current. The Force of Star Wars performs a similar role: one who taps into this resource (energy, pattern, mindset, law, principle, etc.) is rendered far more powerful than they would be without it. Of course, while some of the abilities conferred by the Force are more spectacular than those conferred by Tao (such as moving objects with your mind), Taoists have been reputed to do pretty amazing things as well.

Taoism's principal holy book is the *Tao Te Ching*. Although it was originally popularized in English as "The Book of the Way and its Power," most modern translations retain the original Chinese title. That's because it's quite difficult to capture the actual meaning in English. A more accurate title might be "The Book of the Organizing Force and Pattern of the Universe, and the Way it Can be Manifested in Human Society." Not terribly catchy, of course. Then again, Star Wars' original title was "The Adventures of Luke Starkiller," which, let's be honest, isn't so hot either. But what's in a name?

In fact, the very notion of names and language and their limitations feature rather prominently in the *Tao Te Ching*. The very first verse starts off by informing us that the words we use to describe Tao are not really adequate, and that by extension, this entire book shouldn't be taken too literally. That's because one cannot truly understand the Tao through words, but only by living in accordance with it.

Sound familiar? Sounds like something Star Wars' Jedi Master Yoda would say:

> Luke: But how am I to know the good side from the bad?
> Yoda: You will know. When you are calm, at peace. Passive.

Or:

> Luke: What's in there?
> Yoda: Only what you take with you.

Yoda is probably the world's most adorable and famous caricature of an eastern mystic—sort of a mix of Kermit the Frog and Mister Miyagi from the Karate Kid. Like the stereotypical foreign sage, he even speaks in an exotic syntax. His suggestions to Luke and others often sound like the sorts of things you'd find on a fortune cookie, and yet are actually profound and practical bits of advice.

Most of Yoda's teaching deals with the way in which our will gets in the way of our want, and vice versa—it is by struggling too hard to do things that we fail in our attempts to do them. It's only when we let go of expectations that we can act gracefully and freely enough to achieve what needs to be done. In contrast with the western mindset, which often counsels a bullish and stubborn determination to win at all costs, Yoda's take on the Tao (and the Force) is that this ultimately leads to bad results, both for society and for the practitioners themselves. Moreover, the attitude would be prone to end in failure, as the agent would be working against the universe (which is bigger and endlessly resourceful) rather than alongside it.

In order to show the congruence of the Tao of Taoism and the Force of Jediism, I've taken my own translation/interpolation of the *Tao Te Ching* and rewritten it in accordance with elements found in *Star Wars* (mainly the original trilogy). Aside from the obvious (swapping out Tao for the Force, and sage for Jedi), I've reworked some of the other passages to allude more directly to the films, and where appropriate, I've inserted actual lines from Obi Wan Kenobi, Yoda and others (see if you can find them all!). However, despite these modifications, the book still reads as a pretty clear version of the *Tao Te Ching*—certainly more so than my other pop-culture interpretation, *The Dude De Ching* (a mashup with the Coen Brothers' film *The Big Lebowski*), which introduces a surreal aspect all its own.

Please note that my version of the *Tao Te Ching*, upon which this book is based, is rather different than most others. Instead of trying to stick too closely to the original translation, I've attempted to make the meaning of each verse as clear as possible, which occasionally requires reinterpreting the text a bit or adding a few lines not found in the original. I'm not the first to take creative liberties in this way—in fact, others have veered much farther from strict translation. My objective, however, is not to be creative, but rather to make the book's philosophy and ideas immediately comprehensible. Although some look at the *Tao Te Ching* as a mystical, otherworldly text, I believe it makes more sense as a highly practical guide to living well and getting along in the ordinary world.

To learn more about Taoism, please read the appendix at the end of this book, taken from my original *Tao Te Ching*. By explicitly outlining the principles of Taoism, it can help to illuminate the congruence between Taoism and Jediism.

May the Force (and the Tao) be with you,

Additional Notes

If you would like to be ordained for free as a Jedi minister you can do so at The Ministry of Jediism: www.ism.co/jediism. It's fast, free and easy.

The original *Tao Te Ching* upon which *The Tao of the Jedi* is based is available for download as a free ebook at www.ism.co/library/daoism. There is also a link on that page to a longer, annotated version available for purchase at Amazon.com which contains essays explaining each verse.

Male pronouns are often used in this book to signify human beings in general, rather than resorting to awkward grammatical constructions like "he or she." No masculine bias is intended. The anonymous people alluded to could be either female or male.

If you'd like to discuss this book with the author and others, please visit www.ism.co/forums/jediism. Corrections, suggestions, additions and criticisms are most welcome!

THE VERSES

1

The Force that can be discussed is not the true Force.
Things in the galaxy are only temporary reflections of the Force.
The flow of the Force is all that really exists.
Our names and ideas and categories
Are only mind tricks we use to make sense of it.

In order to understand this, one has to first learn how to relax,
In order to experience this, one has to first learn how to unlearn.
The galaxy is made of and by the Force,
And the Force gives rise to all the creativity in the galaxy.

The Force and the physical world may seem separate
But that is only because we are wired to see it that way.
To operate in greater harmony with the Force,
And with the world around us,
We must begin to internalize this way and its perspective.
This is our first step into a larger world.

2

Once beauty is identified as precious,
Ugliness is seen everywhere.
Once the rare is held up as an ideal,
The commonplace is considered bad.

Your focus determines your reality:
Difficult and easy,
Long and short,
High and low,
Sound and silence,
Large and small,
Before and after—
Each of them are complementary parts of a bigger unity,
But our conditioned minds don't perceive it that way.
We drive each aspect as far apart as possible from its complement,
And increasingly obsess over their division.

Therefore, the Jedi acts without struggle or coercion
And teaches by example and allusion rather than rote and rule.
Things come and he welcomes them.
Things go and he bids them farewell.
He helps with no expectation of gain,
Works with no expectation of reward,
Performs with no anticipation of results,
Completes projects but takes no credit.

Since the Jedi takes nothing from the galaxy,
The galaxy takes nothing from him.
And his influence upon it long endures.

3

Exalting superiors invites competition.
Treasuring things that are difficult to obtain encourages theft.
Flaunting objects of desire gives rise to jealousy.

So the Jedi rules by:
Relaxing the people's hearts,
Satisfying their needs,
Lessening their wants,
And strengthening their character.
He trains them to let go of everything they fear to lose.

Once he has shown the people how to live without craftiness and envy,
Cunning interlopers cannot take advantage of nor trick them.
Rooting out unnecessary objectives allows us to live in harmony with
nature.

4

The Force is an empty vessel
Yet everything comes from it.
Though utterly fathomless,
It gives rise to everything we perceive

It smooths sharp edges,
It unties the knots,
It softens the glare,
And settles the dirt of daily life.
Profoundly patient,
It seems to have been around forever.
No one knows where it came from.
This is because it preceded all form and division.

5

The Force is unsentimental—
It treats the living no different than it treats debris.
Jedi are the same: They evaluate everyone impartially.

The Force is like a bellows—
It is empty and yet everything springs from it.
The more pressure put on it, the more it creates.
Man is not like this—
The more he produces, the more exhausted he becomes.

To tap into the Force, the Jedi instead turns inward.
There he finds its calm and creative source
At the very center of his being.

6

The universal Force which gives rise to all life
Can be thought of as a mysterious sort of womb.
The entrance to this profound mother is the origin of the galaxy.
Her presence stretches in all directions, across all time and space.
She seems to give birth without exerting the slightest effort.

7

Why is the Force eternal and enduring?
Because it does not have any ends.
Because it lacks any goals,
The Force can never fail to succeed.

Understanding this,
The Jedi also refuses to contend or compete.
By placing himself in the back,
He soon finds himself out in front.
Because he doesn't have any expectations,
He doesn't suffer any disappointments.
Thus, it is only because he lacks any self-interest
That his interests are fulfilled.

8

It is best to be like the Force
The Force benefits all things,
Yet it does not contend, nor struggle to do so.
The Force naturally goes places shunned by most people.
Even wretched hives of scum and villany.
Because it dwells even in low places, it is of benefit to all—
Even the unpopular and rejected.

Be like the Force:
Dwell modestly, close to the earth,
Penetrate deeply, and reflect serenely upon your environment,
Benefit and nourish all the things around you,
Clearly and faithfully, you should communicate.
When taking charge, be appropriate,
When serving others, be able,
Do not rush nor tarry.
There is a unique time, rhythm and speed for every action.
You already know that which you need.

The Jedi does not pit himself against the Force.
Therefore he never finds his path obstructed by it.

9

The ambitious are oriented toward excess,
But greed puts a strain on systems,
Destroying them.

An overused lightsaber will run out of power
An overflowing vault will be vanquished.
An overvalued ego will be brought down.

Do what is necessary, take what you need,
And then get out of the way.
This is the efficient way in which the Force operates,
So the Jedi follows its example.

10

Can you embrace both the invisible Force and the material world
And see them as two sides of the same oneness?
This will help you maintain integrity
And avoid internal contradiction.

Meditating upon, and subtilizing your inner energy
Allows you to become as pure and receptive as a newborn.
Examining your perceptions of the galaxy
Allows you to cleanse them of all dust and distortion.
Your eyes can deceive you. Don't trust them.
Instead, stretch out with your feelings.

Identifying with the people over whom you have influence
Prevents you from being distracted by your own self-interest.
As temptations avail themselves to you
Can you remain steadfast as a mother porg in her nest?
As you grow wise and knowledgeable about many things,
Can you retain the modesty of a Padawan?

Both the Force and the Jedi nurture the people
Without assuming any ownership of them.
They act without expecting results,
And lead without controlling.
Human beings call this virtue.
It is the very embodiment of the Force—
The Force manifesting itself through the human heart.

11

A humble dwelling is constructed from clay and straw,
Yet it is the emptiness inside which makes it a home.
A cup may be cut from the finest crystal,
Yet it is the hollow at its center which allows one to drink.
A starship may be fashioned from duralloy and ferroceramic,
Yet it is the vacant area inside which affords us its value.

Therefore, although presence provides identity,
Empty space affords utility.

12

Be mindful of your feelings:
Too much light blinds the eye,
Too much sound deafens the ear,
Too much spice blunts the taste,
Too much excitement maddens the mind,
Too much desire compromises the character.

That is why the Jedi puts his inner needs first,
By moderating the external distractions of the senses.

13

The Jedi say:
"Both praise and blame induce anxiety, for honors are fleeting and fickle."
We indulge our anxieties because they safeguard the self.
It seems that consternation may be a condition of consciousness.

However,
For those who regard themselves as a part of a much greater whole,
Praise and blame no longer elicit unease.
Undivided from environment,
They care about their surroundings as much as they care about themselves.

This is why it is only those who see themselves as ordinary
Who may be fit to influence the galaxy,
And only those immune to honor
Who may actually deserve it.

14

You can look for the Force, but it cannot be seen.
You can listen for the Force, but it cannot be heard.
You can grasp for the Force, but it cannot be touched.
When something is incapable of being sensed or categorized or measured
in this way,
It is because it is not a thing—
It is an undifferentiated field of potential.

Though it has both light and dark sides,
The Force itself is neither light nor dark.
Rather, it foreshadows the very division of opposites,
And thus it is impossible to define.
It emerges only to vanish again and again.
We might consider it a formula for the unformed,
An illustration of the undefined,
An outline of ambiguity.

Don't try to examine it directly,
You won't make any sense of it.
Rather, practice being one with the Force in the here-and-now.
In doing this, you will share in its momentum—
An unimpeded unfolding
Which started back at the beginning of all things.

15

The ancient Jedi were masters of making their way in the world.
Since we can scarcely comprehend the depths of their understanding,
All we can do is reflect upon their outward attitude:

Careful, like a man crossing a frozen stream,
Vigilant, like someone surrounded on all sides by threat,
Courteous, like an honored guest,
Yielding, like thawing ice,
Unassuming, like uncarved wood,
Receptive, like an empty valley,
Yet incomprehensible as a turbid pool.

Muddy water once settled becomes clear,
And settled water once again becomes agitated.
The Jedi who can remain steadfast and avoid the vicissitudes of excess,
Avoids becoming buffeted by changing currents,
And naturally cleaves to the path between them,
The one which cuts right through.

16

Maintain a perfect stillness,
And you will witness everything arising from this quietude.
Rising and falling,
Like your breath,
Everything without fail returns to the void.

When you are able to see that everything returns to the void,
You will have gained insight into the human condition.
Prior to attaining this insight,
You are under the constant risk of compulsive behavior,
And compulsive behavior can ruin your life.

When you attain this insight into the nature of things,
You will learn to embrace the entire world.
By embracing the entire world you will become profoundly unbiased.
By being profoundly unbiased you will become deeply selfless.
By being deeply selfless you will become one with the Force.
And the Force protects its own.

17

The greatest Jedi are barely known,
The next best are admired,
The next best are feared,
The next best are loathed.
The stronger the feelings, the weaker the trust,
And those who cannot trust, cannot be taught.

Thus, the best Jedi take no credit for their achievements.
This makes the people feel as if they have liberated themselves.

18

When people abandon the Force,
Doctrines of morality and rectitude take its place.

Once intellect and knowledge are esteemed,
Hypocrisy and pretense become routine.

As family relationships become strained,
We start to hear a lot about the importance of kinship.

And it is only when the whole political system is in trouble,
That the senators start preaching about patriotic loyalties.

19

To help humanity:
Spurn holiness,
Discard cleverness,
Abandon the doctrine of righteousness,
And relinquish moral duty.
After rejecting these external injunctions,
A natural piousness and compassion will be allowed to flourish.

Moreover, if we:
Disregard academic knowledge,
And spurn ceremony,
We will be freed from anxiety over status,
And distress over details.

Furthermore, when we:
Root out artifice,
And banish profiteers,
Hustlers and thieves will be obliged to find their targets elsewhere.

However, these are just outward policies.
Within ourselves we must also come to:
Value the unadorned,
Embrace simplicity,
Reduce self-consciousness,
And curtail our craving.
To do this, the Jedi must have the deepest commitment,
The most serious mind.

20

Abandon learning—it brings only sorrow.
How can we tell the good side from the bad side?
Must we fear what others fear?
Fear leads to anger, anger leads to hate, and hate leads to suffering.
The limit to our ignorance is endless.
We can only learn when we are calm, at peace. Passive.

However,
There is endless joy to be had!
The galaxy is endlessly abundant.

The Master watches it all from a distance,
Calm, alone, and expressionless as an unborn infant,
With nothing to do, and nowhere to go.

The people indulge in an embarrassment of riches,
While the Master appears to have nothing.
The people seem sharp and clear-minded,
Whereas the Master acts mysteriously.
The people appear confident and assertive,
But the Master looks disheveled and withdrawn.
The people take pride in being gainfully employed,
While the Master remains stubbornly idle.

The Master appears foolish, even somewhat rude.
Aimless as the restless winds,
He seems to have little direction at all.

Though the Master is different from everyone else,
He is content.
Everything he needs is right in front of him.

21

Human virtue is an expression of the Force,
Yet the path to its door is elusive and indistinct.

Forms and patterns may be latent within the Force,
But they are obscured to us, mysterious.
The essence of life springs from it,
Yet we can't observe the fountainhead.
We only know of the Force from its predicates:
A ceaseless flow of creativity from ancient times until now.

This succession from the Force endures—
Its chain of manifestations have persevered through history.
We too are a product of that lineage,
So how we can follow the Force, and manifest its virtue?
Only by searching within ourselves,
And locating the links.

22

Only that which is humbled can be improved.
Only that which is broken can be attended to.
Only that which is emptied can be filled up.
Only that which is worn out can be rejuvenated.
Only one who possesses little can ever hope to be satisfied—
This is why those who clutch at success, wealth and status
Come to feel as if deprived.

Therefore, in order that he can help balance the galaxy,
The Jedi embraces a unity of opposites.
In order to attend to its totality,
He does not focus on himself.

By not claiming to be right,
He becomes righteous.
By not admiring himself,
He merits admiration.
By not being arrogant,
He emerges as a natural leader.
It is only because he does not fight with the galaxy,
That the whole galaxy fights alongside him.

The ancient Jedi said, "He who surrenders, wins."
This was not just a clever saying.
He who humbles himself,
Finds a fount of power within,
And a world of welcome without,
So he is able to overcome anything.

23

Nature doesn't dwell on things,
Therefore its violence doesn't perpetuate itself—
Its cyclones peter out,
Its rainstorms lash and then depart.
Even if we wanted to exacerbate Nature's tumult, we could not.
Therefore one who comports themselves in a natural way,
Will spontaneously adopt the quiet virtue of nature,
Just as one who opposes naturalness,
Will find themselves ever buffeted by turmoil.

Man is but an extension of nature,
Therefore he who lives in accordance with it
Helps to extend its patterns onto the galaxy.
In so doing, he acts as an agent for the Force.

The converse is also true:
One who behaves unnaturally
Acts as an impediment to the Force
And hinders its unfolding.

24

Stand on your tiptoes and you will fall over.
Overextend your stride and you will tire quickly.
Focus on yourself and you will never learn anything.
Sit stubbornly and you will never move forward.
Admire yourself and you will never be admired.
In this way, the universe self-corrects itself,
And prevents the selfish from persevering.

From the point of view of the Force,
Excessive and greedy actions are like tumors.
This is why people naturally detest them.
Because he follows the Force,
A Jedi rejects them as a matter of principle.

25

There is something completely nebulous
That predated the galaxy.
Tranquil, formless and solitary,
It persists as it provides,
Like some vast cosmic mother.
We can't compartmentalize it,
So we just refer to it as "The Force."

However, if we were compelled to try to describe it,
We might call it great, all-pervasive, and far-reaching,
Something which comes from the origin of all things,
Surrounds and penetrates everything,
And returns to the origin of all things.
It binds the galaxy together.
It is the power of greatness which makes all great things greater:
Nature, the galaxy, humanity, and leaders of men.

People often forget that there are entities greater than their leaders:
While leaders follow the laws of humanity,
Humanity follows the laws of the galaxy,
The galaxy follows the laws of nature,
Nature follows the laws of the Force,
And the Force follows itself.
Everything follows from this.

26

The extremes of creation and recreation entail each other,
Like those of tranquility and tension.

The Jedi walks all day,
But never abandons his cargo.
Even though there are magnificent sights to distract him,
He remains calm and single-minded.
It is only when his duty is done
That he can go back to being unconcerned and aloof.

Similarly, a great ruler cannot indulge in frivolity,
Else she will lose her focus.
And she cannot allow herself to abandon her self-control,
Else she will lose all control.

27

A good traveler leaves no trace,
A good speaker leaves no doubt,
A good adventurer needs no odds,
A well-locked door needs no barricade,
A well-tied knot needs no reinforcement.

The Jedi tirelessly supports those in need
Without stepping on the toes of others.
He helps all,
Without rejecting anyone, nor anything.
It takes a special kind of wisdom to act in this way.
For the truly good person, his goodness will never be exhausted.
By guiding those who require his service,
And sharing what he has with the bereft,
He only increases his own store of goodness.

Conversely, the Padawan who does not respect his teacher,
And who does not cherish his lesson,
Even if he is wise,
Will find himself no better off.

One cannot acquire anything
When they maintain no open place to put it.

28

Respect power,
But maintain receptivity.
By being receptive, one lies underneath the world,
And protects the power of its undifferentiated potential.

To understand the brilliant,
One must also be steeped in the obscure.
By acting as a facilitator for the world,
One gains access to its resources,
Along with its undifferentiated potential.

The Jedi understands glory and honor,
But still clings to humility.
By putting himself beneath the world,
He helps sustain the world,
And safeguards its undifferentiated potential.
The Jedi knows how to turn the Force into a practical means of power,
So great societies are careful to make efficient use of them.

29

Those who want to bend the galaxy to their will,
Will surely fail.
The natural way of things should not be tampered with.
For when one tries to divert it, one destroys it,
And when one tries to grip it, one fumbles it.

Sometimes things move forward,
Sometimes they fall behind,
Sometimes they heat up,
Sometimes they grow cold,
Sometimes they strengthen,
Sometimes they weaken,
Sometimes they overcome,
Sometimes they succumb.

Therefore the Jedi is skeptical of extremes,
And opposed to extravagant ideals.
When arrogance is avoided,
Achievements come naturally, easily, and each within their own time.

30

In knowing and teaching the ways of the Force,
The Jedi eschews the use of aggression,
For he knows it will only incur retaliation.
Where armies encamp, only thorny bushes will grow.
Great wars are followed by famine.
The work of a peacekeeper
Is to make sure that conflict does not arise.

However, when fighting cannot be avoided,
The Jedi does only what is necessary,
And halts immediately thereafter.

He does not seek power for its own sake,
He achieves success but is not arrogant,
He is resolute but not proud,
He fights only with reluctance,
He overcomes without tormenting his opponent.

Though violence may bring about a quicker triumph,
It will also sow the seeds of disaster.
Annihilation runs contrary to the fertility of the Force,
And thus culminates in catastrophe.

31

Military instruments portend peril.
This is why they are naturally feared.
Because they are tools of aggression,
The Jedi holds no affinity for them.

In ordinary affairs, the Jedi gives precedence to inclusion.
It is only in wartime that he elects the path of exclusion.
Thus military instruments do not further the development of
wholesomeness.
Rather, they are a necessary but unfortunate regression in the grand
scheme of things.

The Jedi employs his weapons only as a last resort
And is never enthusiastic about it.
Wars do not make one great,
For to delight in war is to delight in death,
And he who delights in death,
Will himself become subsumed by it.

Thus, when forced into battle,
One should bitterly mourn the massacre of one's adversaries,
And commemorate victory not with a celebration,
But with a wake.

32

The Force is eternal and absolute,
Yet in its nameless, potential, and undifferentiated state,
It exerts little influence upon the world.

No one in the world can harness it wholly.
If only the rulers of the world could master it,
Then everything would naturally fall into place,
All our problems would be solved,
The people would be perfectly content,
And they would no longer need to be governed to get along.

Civilization gives rise to institutions,
And the habit of categorizing things,
Yet we need to recognize the limits of their efficacy:
To mark boundaries is to impose barriers upon the world.

Why is this important?
Because the way the Force manifests in the world
Is analogous to streams joining together into a great river
And those rivers uniting into an all-encompassing ocean.

33

It takes wit to understand other people,
But it takes humility to understand oneself.
It takes power to conquer other people,
But it takes resilience to conquer oneself.

Wealth arises not from riches,
But from lack of want.
Thus he who categorically accepts his lot in life,
Is wealthy beyond measure,
And his impact upon the world, immense.

34

The Force flows everywhere and in all directions.
Everything in the galaxy relies upon it,
Yet it doesn't expect anything in return.

It works diligently,
Yet seeks no merit.
It is all-powerful,
Yet seeks no control.
It is eternal,
Yet seeks no sustenance.
Thus it can be found amongst even the most insignificant.
It provides the ground for all things,
Yet requires no tithe.
Thus it can be placed among the greatest of the great.

In the same way,
The Jedi does not seek greatness.
This is how he finds it.

35

To one who can grasp the idea of the Force,
The entire world makes itself available,
So no harm can come to him—
Only joy, abundance and contentment.

Though music and sweets may tantalize the typical passerby,
The Force is silent, and as transparent and tasteless as water.
Thus it is often ignored.

If you look for the Force you will not see it,
If you listen for the Force you will not hear it,
But if you learn to make use of it,
It will be of use to you always.

36

That which is stretched too far will snap back.
That which uses too much power will become enfeebled.
That which is built up too high will topple over.
That which is overloaded with riches will soon be raided.

The weak will eventually overcome the strong—
This principle reveals the value of humility.
Just as fish who rise up to the surface are consumed,
Strength, when vaunted, is vanquished.

37

The Force doesn't do anything,
And yet somehow it gets everything done.
If the mighty could also eschew objectives,
Everything in society would naturally thrive.

When objectives assert themselves,
They can be subdued with simplicity.
Subdued by simplicity, tranquility is attained,
And society once again thrives as it may.

38

Jedi of the highest character do not think about virtue,
Which is why they are the most virtuous,
While those of lower character strive to attain virtue,
Which is why they rarely do.
Furthermore, those who try especially hard to be virtuous
Often become unwitting instruments of the dark side.

The truly virtuous
Act without objective,
And thus have no need to be recognized.

Beneath the virtuous,
The benevolent are moved by a code of valor,
And so must strive after honor and accolade.
Yet at least they do not impose morality upon others.

Beneath the benevolent,
The righteous perceive themselves as moral guardians,
And so must strive to control and command.
Yet at least they are concerned with the living.

Beneath the righteous,
The holy are only interested in tradition and ritual.
Since no one really cares about any of that,
They must strive to establish their doctrines through violence.

Thus,
When The Force is turned away from, we hear about virtue,
When virtue is lost, we hear about benevolence,
When benevolence is lost, we hear about morality,
And when morality is lost, we hear about historical imperatives.

It follows that:
Of all the methods to find the way in the galaxy,
Hewing to traditional doctrine is by far the shabbiest,
And a portent of great troubles to come.

Any presumed wisdom is like a petal
On an enormous and unfolding tree of knowledge.
Mistaking the flower for the tree itself
Renders the system infertile,
Nurturing only ignorance and delusion.

This is why the Jedi
Concern themselves with the pith instead of the peel,
The fruit instead of the flower,
The trunk instead of the twigs.
Electing sustenance, they shed the superficial.

39

In ancient times everything was unified by the Force.
Because of this:
The sky was clear,
Societies were settled,
The air was energized,
The rivers were abundant,
Nature flourished,
And rulers could govern virtuously.

But without this unity:
The sky collapses,
Society sinks,
The air dissipates,
The rivers dry up,
Everything weakens,
And rulers are laid low.

Thus to achieve nobility,
One must recognize a dependence upon the humble.
To reach great heights,
Roots must be tended to assiduously.
To win enduring support,
Great leaders must openly exhibit their humanity.

There is weakness in power, and power in weakness—
Rather being than shiny and precious as jewels,
Be common and steadfast as stone.

40

The Force travels everywhere,
But always returns to its origin,
Though it gives rise to everything in the galaxy,
It does so with enormous gentleness and humility.
This is because it starts from nothing.

41

When the best students learn about the Force,
They work hard to put it into practice.
When mediocre students learn about the Force,
They practice it only half-heartedly.
When the worst students learn about the Force,
They laugh it up!
This is how we know it is truly the Force:
When the nerf-herders find it hilarious.

Thus it is said that while starting on the path of the Force:
The way of illumination appears dark,
Moving forward seems like a retreat,
The easier way appears more difficult,
The highest virtue sounds hollow,
The purest innocence looks disgraced,
The wisest mind seems ignorant,
The most steadfast character appears deceitful,
The most evident truth seems spurious,
The ideal structure looks badly-shaped,
The perfect tool takes too long to implement,
The finest music is too unsettling to enjoy,
The most beautiful image betrays no evident form.

The Force is utterly obscure and unnamable.
This is how it safeguards its power,
And how it is able to invest itself so effectively in the world.

42

The Force gives rise to a unified field of being,
The unified field of being splits into the dark and the light,
The interplay of dark and light gives birth to creativity,
And creativity produces all the things we perceive in the world.

Elements in the galaxy are vehicles for dark and light,
Helping to blend their vital energies.

Most people hate to be low and disrespected,
Yet the Jedi can see the value in being an outsider.
They know that in certain conditions
Loss can be a gain, and gain can be a loss.

In order alleviate their suffering,
The disrespected often embrace the dark side.
Instead, the Jedi learns to embrace his suffering
In order to pass through to the light.

It's been said many times before:
Those who visit violence upon the world
Will surely have violence visited upon them.
The menace of the dark side is a vicious circle.
It is the most important thing in the world there is to understand.

43

The softest things in the galaxy,
In time, naturally overcome the hardest.
The most formless things in the galaxy,
In time, naturally overcome the most solid.

From these examples we can learn the value of not trying.
Do. Or do not. There is no try.

Of course, this can be very difficult to understand—
How it is that passivity can lead to success.

44

Status or self-regard, which is more significant?
Well-being or wealth, which is worth more?
Gain or loss, which incurs more pain?

The greater the attachment, the more acute the suffering.
The greater the hoard, the more damaging the loss.

The Jedi is immune to disappointment.
Since he does not covet, he incurs no danger.
Incurring no danger, he lives long and thrives.

45

The greatest accomplishment may appear ordinary,
But its greatness lies in its eternal utility.
The greatest abundance may appear unimpressive,
But its greatness lies in its inexhaustibility.

Similarly,
The straightest lightsaber may seem skewed,
The deepest ideas may appear hokey,
And the greatest wisdom may sound foolish and ungrammatical.
Yet the truths we cling to depend greatly on our own point of view.

Movement will overcome cold.
Stillness will overcome heat.
To help bring equilibrium to the world,
Be mindful of your feelings,
And the world will flourish
Despite any of your efforts to understand it.

46

When the light side of the Force prevails,
Banthas are free to fertilize the fields.
When the dark side of the Force washes over,
Banthas are repurposed as weapons of warfare.

Nature is an amoral system,
It is when we aid or hinder its flow
That its fruit is rendered fertile or fallow.

There is no curse more deep-rooted than dissatisfaction,
And no affliction more self-stoking than greed,
For only when we learn how to cultivate contentment,
Can we hope to become a friend to the Force.

47

The whole galaxy can be understood
Without leaving your room.
The Force can be witnessed
Without looking out your window.

The further one progresses,
The less one understands.

Therefore the Jedi:
Doesn't look, yet perceives
Doesn't seek, yet finds
Doesn't try, yet does—
There is no try.

48

In embracing knowledge, there is a daily augmenting.
In embracing the Force, there is a daily diminishing.
The Jedi tries less and less,
Until all action unfolds without objective.
Though he appears to do very little at all,
Everything important is ultimately achieved.

To do the work of the world,
The Jedi does not wrestle with it.
He who obstructs its natural flow,
Will only find himself pushed aside.

49

The Jedi has no fixed ideas about anything,
So he takes in a broad range of information—
Not only from the admired,
But also from the shunned,
And so doubles the value he receives.
He entertains not only the credible,
But also the incredible,
And so multiplies his libraries of learning.

To help bring balance to the Force,
The Jedi draws people together into one big glorious muddle.
In this way, he prevents the birth of bias.

Like organisms cut off from their ecosystem,
Isolated perceptions become dry, brittle and dead.

50

Though death is a natural part of life,
Our attachment to life leads to fear, anger and suffering.
Humans deal with this in various ways—
Three in ten follow the dark side of the Force,
Three in ten follow the light side,
And three in ten are so afraid of dying,
That they never truly live at all.

However,
The one in ten who is truly adept at living long and well
Does not fear wild creatures,
Nor soldiers on the battlefield.
Horns and claws do not rend his flesh,
And lightsabers do not pierce his heart.
Why is this?
Because he studies both the light and dark sides of the Force.

51

The Force itself brings forth life,
While the channeling of the Force helps nurture it.
What we call virtue is the channeling of the Force.

Things take shape according to their inner nature,
And environment helps perfect them.
This is why everything in the galaxy esteems the Force,
And glorifies virtue.
Yet the Force's esteem and virtue's glory,
Are not bestowed upon them.
Rather, they arise naturally.

The Force provides life and nurtures it,
Rears and nourishes it,
Shelters and matures it,
Sustains and protects it.

Though the Force gives life,
It does so without any hint of possessiveness.
It assists without any expectation of return.
It mentors without imposing its authority.

These are the greatest virtues imaginable,
And so the Jedi incorporates them in all his actions.

52

The progenitor of the galaxy
May be thought of as its mother.
You must first learn to fathom the mother
In order to understand the children.
Then, once the children are made sense of,
You can return to the maternal bosom
And she will protect you from all the peril in the world.

Temper your senses,
Cultivate restraint,
And you will enjoy a life of peace.

Alternatively,
Keep your mouth always open,
Multiply your activities,
And you will invite all the trouble in the galaxy.
Adventure, excitement—
The Jedi craves not these things.

Size matters not:
Cherishing the insignificant
Reveals great profundity.
Aligning with the fragile
Confers great strength.
This will help safeguard you from misfortune.
Use the Force to illuminate evidence rather than doctrine.
It is the practice which shines light upon the dark.

53

If we had the tiniest bit of sense,
We would always be with the Force,
Avoiding distractions and dangers.
Its light side is broad and smooth,
Yet for some odd reason,
People are prone to veer off into the darkness.

Though the mighty grow more powerful,
The poor fields lie fallow,
The elite wear elegant clothes,
With fine jewels dangling upon them.
They eat and drink excessively,
Enjoying riches too innumerable to apprehend,
While their subjects stagnate and suffer.
In any other context, this would be considered grand larceny.
While the powerful may consider this a bright and noble path,
It is a road which leads directly to darkness.

54

That which is given a good foundation in the Force,
Cannot be knocked down.
That which deeply embraces the Force,
Cannot be divorced from it.
The Force's adepts are heirs to its homestead,
Just as children are kin to their clan.

When one cultivates the Force in his person,
His character will become genuine.
When one cultivates the Force in his family,
Its strength will become multiplied.
When one cultivates the Force in his community,
Its virtue will become long-lasting.
When one cultivates the Force in his nation,
Its goodness will prosper.
When one cultivates the Force everywhere,
Its benefits will spread broadly across the galaxy.

To get started,
Compare your person against other persons,
Compare your family against other families,
Compare your community against other communities,
Compare your nation against other nations,
And compare your world with everything that has come before it.

How can one confirm that this method works?
Only through personal observation.
The most difficult trial a Jedi must face
Is to look inside themselves.
What is in there?
Only what you have taken with you.

55

A Jedi that is rich in character
Can be said to be like a newborn baby.

Like a baby,
Snakes and scorpions will not sting him,
Wild animals will not attack him,
And birds of prey will not swoop down upon him.
His bones are flexible,
And his muscles soft—
Yet his grip is so strong!
He is unaware of coitus,
And yet his penis stands erect—
His vitality is at full potential indeed!
He can scream all day and not become hoarse—
In what great shape his body must be!

To know this freshness is to be in accord with the eternal,
And to be in accord with the eternal is to be enlightened.

Though vitality inevitably wanes,
Artificial attempts at increase are ill-fated.
An overuse of vital energy is bound to backfire:
Those who struggle against their twilight
Grow old before their time.
This is a departure from the way of the Force—
And whatever departs from this way
Meets an untimely end.
Death is a natural part of life.
Rejoice for those around you who transform into the Force.

56

The wise do not preach about wisdom,
Just as those who preach about wisdom are not wise.

Shut your mouth,
Close your eyes,
Blunt your edges,
Untie your knots,
Unwind your intellect,
And identify yourself with the ground.
This is how you become one with the Force.

Once unity with the Force is achieved,
You will no longer be attached, nor aloof,
Nor benefited, nor harmed,
Nor ennobled, nor disgraced.

Luminous beings are we, not crude matter.
A liberation from all expectation—
This is the highest state of human development.

57

Great leaders make forthright plans,
And great generals make deceptive plans,
But the Jedi refuse to make any plans at all—
This is how they guide the world.

How is this a strategy for leadership?
Because the more plans and prohibitions we make,
The more the people grow impoverished.
The more the powerful profit from war and weaponry,
The more the nation grows chaotic.

The more that crafty schemes
Are floated among the populace,
The more things fall apart.
By enacting more laws,
We create more criminals.

Hence the Jedi:
Doesn't insist that anyone change,
Yet the people naturally transform themselves.
He presides peacefully,
Yet the people get along with each other.
He doesn't meddle in their business,
Yet the people prosper.
He expects nothing from them,
Yet the people learn to live with grace.

58

When leaders are unobtrusive,
The people remain sincere.
When leaders interfere with their lives,
The people contend with each other for advantage.

Good fortune follows from bad fortune,
Just as bad fortune follows from good—
No one knows what lies just around the corner.

Thus there is no method that is always correct,
Because what is correct soon deviates into what is incorrect.
Excellence will be beset by the ominous.
This is why the people have always struggled to figure out how to live—
Because the future is impossible to see.

So the Jedi cultivates a sharp wit,
But does not use it to cut dullards down.
He speaks honestly, but does not insult.
He deals directly, but does not bully.
Though his wisdom gently illuminates,
It never blinds nor dazzles.
The reason he acts this way
Is because he knows not the destination,
But only the path.

59

In helping the people,
And attending to the environment,
Nothing is greater than humility.
It is by practicing humility,
That the Jedi becomes one with the Force.

The more rapid your return to the Force,
The greater your crop of character.
The greater your crop of character,
The more challenges can be overcome.
The more challenges you overcome,
The more limitless your life.
The more limitless your life,
The greater your capacity to cultivate.
And the greater your capacity to cultivate,
The more profound your influence can be.

This is what happens when one attends ardently to roots—
A flourishing of enduring vitality and vision.

60

The Jedi guides others in the same way
That he would cook a delicate fish:
That is to say, he meddles as little as possible.

When society is led in accordance with the Force,
Ideology no longer finds any purchase.
It's not that ideology loses any allure,
Only that the people no longer require it.

When dominating influences are no longer imposed on the people,
Organic order is welcomed into the world.

61

A great society should be like a lowland delta
Toward which all things flow downstream,
Commingling their potency.

Similarly,
It is by remaining receptive
That the submissive overcomes the dominating.
By attending to the base of things,
Receptivity restores balance in the world.

It is in this way:
That by submitting to the weak,
The strong can win their loyalty,
And that by submitting to the strong,
The weak can win their protection.

Thus, there is enormous power in humbling oneself.
If a relationship is mutually beneficial,
What does it matter who wears the crown?

62

The Force is the source and sanctuary of all things.
It is both the millhouse of the Master,
And the safehouse of the sinner.

Beautiful speech wins adoration,
And honorable acts win respect,
But the disgraced are not without potential—
Why should we cast them aside?

When great rulers are coronated,
They are honored with gifts and jewelry.
Yet these are mere trinkets,
When compared with the fortunes of the Force.

Why has the Force been regarded as the greatest fortune of all?
Because to those who abide in the Force,
The greatest grace is revealed,
And to those who confide in the Force,
The basest disgrace is repealed.

63

The Jedi acts without aggression,
Works without will,
Tastes without prejudice,
Regards the tiny as great,
Sees a dearth as an abundance,
Regards an adversary with sympathy,
Deals with the doable before it grows difficult,
And attends to the minor before it becomes major.

The hardest problems were once thought of as simple,
And the biggest issues started off small.
One who takes responsibilities too lightly
Will never be trusted,
Just as one that regards everything as trivial,
Will soon find it all insurmountable.

It is precisely because the Jedi don't think of themselves highly
That they achieve greatness:
Because they regard everything as important,
They are never caught off guard,
And nothing is ever too difficult for them to do.

64

That which is unmoving is easily grasped.
That which has not yet occurred is easily prevented.
That which is infirm is easily overcome.
That which is delicate is easily dismantled.

The Jedi deals with a problem before it develops,
Takes command of a situation before it spins out of control.

A trunk broader than our embrace
Grows from the slenderest stem.
A tower nine stories high
Ascends from a mere pile of dust.
A journey twelve parsecs long
Begins with a single unit of spacetime.

Struggle with something and you'll break it.
Grasp too tightly and it will flow through your fingers.
Because the Jedi doesn't strive,
They don't destroy anything.
And because they don't hold on too hard,
They don't lose anything either.

Ordinary people often ruin things
Just before they're about to complete them.
If you remain as unattached at the end as you are at the beginning,
Your expectations won't get the better of you.

Therefore the Jedi seeks freedom from desire,
And does not prize things that are hard to come by.
In learning how to unlearn what they have learned,
They uncover treasures that others pass over.
In offering these gifts without pressure,
The Jedi helps the world return to its true nature.

65

In ancient times,
Leaders did not try to make people wise.
Instead they employed their wisdom
To sustain the simplicity of the people.
The reason they governed this way
Is because a group cannot be cohesive
When everyone thinks they're smarter than everyone else.

Life is more complicated now,
So the people learn to be complicated.
The Jedi still teach simplicity,
Although few listen to them.

However,
Complicating a culture can destroy a society,
While simplifying its notions can help it stick together.
One who understands how and when to use these two methods
Understands how to bind elements in a group.
And one who understands how to bind elements in a group
Wields the greatest power in the world—
It is a creative power so far-reaching
That it leads back to the very origin of things.

66

What makes the rivers so noble and respected
Is that they skillfully adopt the lower position.
This is why the fertile valleys all flourish around them.

In the same way:
The Jedi who want to lift up the people,
Must place themselves below.
To be the face of the populace,
They must be utterly self-effacing.
To lead, they must place themselves behind.

In this way,
Though the Jedi operate from above,
The people do not feel their weight.
Though they stand out in front,
They do not block the way.
It is because their needs do not contend with anyone else
That there is no reason for anyone to contend with the Jedi.

67

Though everyone knows that the Force is great,
It appears utterly confounding.
Of course, it is only because it is confounding
That it can remain so great—
If its meaning could be easily picked apart,
It would have long ago lost its value!

Here are the three great virtues for the Jedi to treasure:
The first is compassion,
The second is moderation,
The third is humility.

Compassion gives rise to courage,
Moderation gives rise to prosperity,
And humility gives rise to cooperation.

However:
One can be courageous without compassion,
Prosperous without moderation,
And cooperative without humility.
But this goes against the way of the Force,
And so will ultimately lead one to the dark side.

Above all, compassion can accomplish anything:
From winning a battle,
To protecting a populace.
Truly, everything that endures in the galaxy
Is predicated upon, and preserved by compassion.
Compassion is unconditional love,
And unconditional love is central to a Jedi's life.

68

The best warriors are not warlike.
The best pugilists are not pugnacious.
The best contenders are not contentious.
The best overlords do not lord themselves over.

This is called going with the flow of nature—
It is the most effective approach toward dealing with others,
Because it is aligned in accordance with the Force.

69

There is a saying in the military:
Do not be the first to attack.
Rather, focus on holding your ground.
It is better to retreat a foot than to advance an inch.

This is called:
Advancing without movement,
Seizing without grasping,
Confronting without attacking,
And warding off without weaponry.

The greatest error is to disrespect an enemy—
Character is the greatest casualty of conceit.
Thus, when two equal armies collide,
It is the one which laments the need to do so
That is the more likely to triumph.

70

The Master's words are very easy to understand,
And very easy to put into practice,
Yet there are few in the world who understand them,
Or are able to put them into practice.

What the Master teaches involves a process,
Just as a culture involves a curriculum.
It is only because people haven't experienced it directly
That they don't know what he is talking about.

Those who do understand the Master are exceedingly rare,
And so he cherishes them.

Though the Jedi may dress humbly,
They hold luminous treasures within their hearts.

71

Understanding that you don't understand
Is the highest form of understanding.
But not understanding what you think you understand
Is a form of mental illness.

The reason the Jedi don't suffer from this disease
Is because they are trained to diagnose it.

72

The strength of a system
Requires the respect of its members.
Lose their respect, and the system is lost.

Therefore,
Do not encroach upon the territory of others,
And do not reduce their quality of life.
It is only when people are disturbed,
That they are given to creating a disturbance in the Force.

It is for this reason that the Jedi know their strengths,
Yet don't show them off.
Though they have great self-respect,
They do not stoke their self-regard.
By rooting out a sense of superiority,
The Jedi cultivate a strong relationship with their fellows.

73

Like the Force,
Heroism has two sides:
Courage with caution conserves life.
But feats of foolhardiness lead to death.
Bravery can help, or it can hurt
And it's not always easy to anticipate the outcome.
Even the Jedi recognize the difficulty and danger in this.

The Force does not contend,
Yet it conquers.
It does not speak,
And yet it answers.
It does not summon,
And yet it receives.
Though it slacks, it succeeds.
Its web is porous,
And yet nothing falls from its embrace.

74

If people are no longer afraid to die,
Then death will be no deterrent.
They embrace the dark side of the Force
Only when life becomes worse than death.

The dark side is the great executioner,
And death has long been its domain.
But he who assumes the role of the reaper
Ignores the double side of the saber.
Just like getting between a lumberjack and his lumber,
He who puts himself on the path to the dark side
Is prone to be cut down.

Once you start down the dark path
It will dominate your destiny forever.

75

The people are only poor,
Because they've been pillaged by the powerful.
The meek are only a mess,
Because they've been meddled with by the mercenary.
The obedient only obsess over gods and the afterlife,
Because their actual lives have been impaired by their overlords.

Thus, those who take too much from the galaxy
Are adversaries of life, and of the Force,
While those who take only what they need
Are their allies and associates.

76

At birth, man is supple and soft,
At death, he is stiff and brittle.
When full of life, grasses and trees are flexible and soft,
But approaching death they are withered and dry.
Thus, the hard and stubborn is the disciple of death,
While the pliant and yielding is the disciple of life.

In this way,
A campaign that cannot accommodate will collapse,
Just as a tree that cannot bend will break.
Those who chase the dark side, in standing firm, will be laid low,
While those who champion the light side, in moving, will emerge
ascendant.

77

The Force is like an archer's bow:
As it performs, the high is pulled down,
And the low is raised up.
The way of the Force is to maintain equilibrium:
It saps from surplus,
And replenishes the scarce.

The way of mankind is very different from this:
It takes from those who have too little,
And gives to those who already have too much.

In understanding and respecting the way of the Force,
The Jedi is able to help set things right.
He invests but does not expect any return,
Completes but does not take any credit.
In this way he can act as an instrument without ends
And so his influence will be endless.

78

Nothing in the world is as soft and accommodating as water,
And yet for overcoming the hard and inflexible,
There is nothing more effective.

Everyone knows that the liquid undermines the adamant,
That the yielding wears away at the unyielding,
Yet few of us are able to put this principle into play.

Therefore the Master says:
Only he who can embrace a society's failings
Is qualified to rule its citizens.
And only he who can bear its burden
Deserves to be carried on their shoulders.

These ideas may seem paradoxical at first glance,
But the Force is often like that.

79

After making peace with an adversary
There is usually some lingering enmity.
What can be done about this?

To expedite the accord,
The Jedi will honor their end of the agreement,
But show mercy to the other side.

Whereas the Jedi focuses upon making amends,
The petty are concerned with assigning blame.
The Force itself is objective,
So it rewards only those who see the bigger picture,
And penalizes those who merely pursue personal interest.

80

The ideal society would be small, with a modest population,
And enough resource to amass an army,
Yet no recourse to deploy it.
They would value their lives so much
That they would see no reason to venture from home.

They would maintain vehicles,
Yet have little occasion to ride them.
They would store armaments,
But have little occasion to exhibit them.
They would return to the old ways of doing things:
Enjoying their food,
Taking pride in their appearance,
Feeling secure in their homes,
And venerating the simple life.

Neighboring villages would stand in plain view,
Yet the people would happily pass their whole lives
Without ever having bothered to go visit.

81

Wise language may not be beautiful,
But beautiful language is rarely wise.
The serene do not have much to say,
Yet those who talk a lot are rarely serene.
The deep may not be elegant,
But the elegant are rarely deep.

The Jedi do not hoard—
The more they give,
The more they receive.
The more they help,
The more they succeed.
They work to introduce flow into the world.
To do this, they follow the Force.

The way of the Force is simple:
To benefit without hurting.
Thus the Jedi do not fight nor struggle to do good in the world,
Instead, they elect to do so with the greatest of ease.
In this way, the Force will be with them, always.
The galaxy has brought you here.
Your path, clearly, this is.

Appendix
INTRODUCTION TO TAOISM

By Oliver Benjamin

OVERVIEW

Most of the current world religions were birthed during the same narrow slice of time, about 2500 years ago. According to historians, Buddhism, Taoism, Jainism, Confucianism, and Monotheistic Judaism all arose nearly simultaneously, within the same 50-year span. It's pretty remarkable, especially when you consider that most of these societies were geographically isolated from one another.

Historian Karl Jaspers famously referred to the period between 800 BC and 200 BC the "Axial Age" because it marks a great shift in thinking about life, the universe and everything. Around this time, the rapid rise and spread of civilization across the world encouraged the rise of cities, the commingling of peoples and the growing importance of material wealth and the consequent protection of assets and territory. Aside from the religions mentioned above, this period of change also includes classical Hinduism (about 800 BC) and Greek classicism (470 BC). Although Christianity arrived late (33 or 100 AD), it arose to address the same issues.

In order to provide a mental framework that would help people live in the challenging and alien environment which civilization provided, cultures were forced to come up with new ideas and codes that could help ease the transition—the result of which are our modern religions. Since the problems they were created to address were the same, it follows that so are the essential messages they purvey: Treat other people as you would treat yourself; inner peace can be found by looking within; the world is bigger than you and your immediate kinfolk; don't covet stuff too much; life is precious; don't be egotistical; lighten up. These problems of civilization are still with us today, and consequently, so are those religions.

As with the other Axial Age religions, Taoism arose during a time of turbulence and change, an era in China known as "The Warring States period." The rapid rise in weapons technology brought about by the Iron Age made it possible for warlords to seize vast amounts of territory, putting the mass of population in harm's way. By some estimates over fifty percent of all males were killed in battle or by conquest, with their kin also killed or taken into slavery. Consequently, the sudden race to empire meant that entire cultures were apt to be utterly wiped out by the victors. This was not an easy time to be alive. The famous Chinese curse "May you live in interesting times" certainly applied to this era.

Taoism is considered to have officially begun right in the middle of this period and is believed to have come into being with the writing of this book, the *Tao Te Ching*.

During this era, nearly all the *Ching* (or classic tomes) that were produced were military handbooks meant to advise agitated emperors and armies on tactics and management. Though the *Tao Te Ching* contains some advice for leadership and strategy, on the whole it seems to be diametrically opposed to the temper of the times. That is, it seems more than anything to be a rejection of the violence of the era, and a longing for the simpler way of life that preceded the turmoil.

Legend has it that the author of the *Tao Te Ching*, Lao Tzu was an elderly and revered court librarian, one of the most widely-read and therefore knowledgeable men in the entire country. Appalled by the violence and scheming that had overtaken his people, he decided to leave his comfortable government post and venture out west into the hinterlands to enjoy some semblance of the old way of life.

Upon arriving at the border, an official recognized his name. They chatted, and when the official learned of his plan to leave forever, he pleaded with Lao Tzu to write down the most profound lessons he had gathered in a lifetime of perusing all the scrolls in the imperial library. The old man obliged and before shambling off into the wild unknown, scribbled down the following 81 short passages,

Though picturesque, Taoism's origin story is most likely a fable. Most historians believe that the *Tao Te Ching* was originally composed for the benefit of a head of state as a manual of political governance and strategy[1]. However, it has evolved far beyond that—2500 years later the *Tao Te Ching* is one of the most widely read books in the world, and has been translated more times than any other, apart from the Christian

---

[1] Most historians are highly skeptical about the historical existence of Lao Tzu as well.

Bible. Its message is timeless and beautiful, and for what we now consider a religious book, uniquely free of deities, doctrine and rules of conduct. Rather, it can be interpreted as a series of sympathetic suggestions on how to get the most out of life.

Though history is loaded with books on how to optimize our time here on earth, what makes the *Tao Te Ching* "religious"[2] rather than just folksy or philosophical, is that Lao Tzu suggests that all living systems (biological, social, political, etc.) operate in similar manners, and upon the same principles. Taoism is thus a "metaphysics" in the original ancient Greek sense of the word—not superstition, but a general theory about the organization and dynamics of the world and its systems.

Consequently, for the adherent of Taoism, respecting the optimal "way" of living systems means that if we follow the word's natural patterns, an enhanced quality of life will ensue, both for their individual selves and the societies they are a part of. This is because, according to Lao Tzu, harmony, synthesis, and creativity is the main thrust of the world rather than discord and destruction.[3] By pointing to examples in nature, he endeavored to show that the proof of this is all around us.

Indeed, though the *Tao Te Ching* is the principal holy book of Taoism, it might be said that the true text of Taoism is actually nature itself. After civilization's long push away from a natural environment to which we're genetically adapted[4], we've lost the ability to understand its language. The *Tao Te Ching*, then, can be seen as a sort of translation primer which helps us begin to make sense of nature and its principles.

---

[2] We use the term loosely. "Religious" is a hard term to define. However, prior to the advent of science, a theory that would aim to describe the whole world and its workings would be thought of as religious. Arguably, that is still true today. Any all-encompassing theory about the world is prone to be outside the realms of both science and philosophy, each of which tends to deal with specific particulars rather than global generalities. Perhaps we need a new vocabulary.
[3] Taoism recognizes the necessity of destruction, a continual rising and falling of organized systems as suggested by its iconic symbol the yin/yang. Nevertheless, the net aggregate of Tao's unfolding is growth and synthesis, as evidenced by the existence and continued flourishing of nature and the world itself.
[4] This is the essential message of the findings from the emergent field of Evolutionary Psychology: After about 100,000 years of living in a stable environment in Africa, human minds became adapted to a certain way of life, far more natural and intimate than the one civilized man lives in now. Many of our psychological and social problems result from the incongruity between our adapted minds and our environment. Evolution occurs on a pace too slow to adapt to the way of life that arose 10,000 years ago with the advent of agriculture and sedentary, multifaceted civilization.

THE MEANING OF THE TITLE

In order to understand the book, we might as well first start by making sense of its mysterious Chinese title[5].

Tao is normally translated as the "Way." That is to say, the mysterious yet powerful and generous manner in which the living world unfolds. Prior to the advent of sciences like biology and genetics, the concept of Tao helped explain the bounty, diversity and evolution of the world and its life forms. However, although the advancement of sciences that help explain much about these things today, Tao is still a highly useful and poetic metaphor for the (still mysterious) power and operation of living systems. For those so inclined, the *Tao Te Ching* can operate as a sort of bridge between scientific theories about life, and a philosophical worldview which helps us to understand it on a more personal level.

Te is normally translated as "virtue" but more properly, it refers to the realization of Tao in the world—the vessels and products of its unfolding, the trail that Tao leaves behind. Thus a person brings virtue into the world by acting in accordance with Tao. In short, Te is anything we can perceive which increases the net sum of vitality and flourishing in the world. A loose analogy for the difference between Tao and Te in Taoism might be that of potential and kinetic energy in physics—they are both essentially the same, only one is theoretical and unseen and one is tangible and evident.

Finally, as we've stated, *ching* means something like "book," or more precisely, "foundational text." Thus it follows that the most common translation is something like "The Book of the Way and its Virtue" or "The Book of the Way and its Power." However, since that's so vague and potentially misleading, most modern translations just leave the title untranslated.

Nevertheless, if we were inclined to hazard an illuminative English translation, incorporating what has been stated in this introduction, the title could be rendered as "The book about the way in which life flourishes in the world." This would seem sufficiently grand in scope, and down to earth at the same time, if a bit lengthy. In the end, however,

---

[5] We're not saying the title is mysterious because it's Chinese—it's mysterious in Chinese as well.

rather than break with modern tradition (and risk confusing our audience), I've chosen to stick with the original Chinese title.

Now that we've made some sense of the name of the book, the next step would be to try to understand the principles put forth in the *Tao Te Ching*. This is how the *Tao Te Ching* guides us to apprehend the vague and unfathomable Tao—by pointing out its characteristics and patterns as they occur in natural systems. What follows below is a basic list of principles that appear to pop up again and again in the text. One could identify many more, or even consolidate some of them[6]. After all, there's no canonical way to read or interpret the book. If there were, of course, there would be far fewer translations and interpretations![7]

PRINCIPLES OF THE TAO

Skepticism

Whereas most religions tend to advocate various types of faith, Taoism does more or less the opposite. In the very first chapter, we are presented with the humble and disarming disclaimer that Tao isn't something that can really be written about, but that we're going to try anyway. At other times throughout the book, the text essentially recommends "Don't take our word for this. Look for yourself." Moreover, the character of the sage pops up again and again, not as an all-powerful magician, but as a deeply humble and apparently unsteady hermit, one who is misunderstood and even rejected by the average person. Compare this with the mighty and admired holy men found in other religions, and it's a wonder Taoism gathered any followers at all.

Ultimately, Taoism provides no easy answers. What it does provide is a way of looking at the world that helps us develop our own answers to conflicts or issues. We can't know Tao (the ideal way of being), but the *Tao Te Ching* suggests that we can learn about it and understand it by appreciating and emulating its aspects, the ones listed here, principles which allow and encourage the world (and ourselves) to flourish.

---

[6] We might consider adding: impartiality, discernment, receptiveness, resourcefulness, gentleness, inclusiveness, and many more.

[7] Also, were Tao able to be nailed down, it wouldn't have its flexibility, breadth or depth. As it says in chapter 41: *Tao is utterly obscure and unnamable. That is how it safeguards its power. And how it is able to invest itself so effectively in the world.*

Non-coerciveness

One of the most important concepts in the *Tao Te Ching* is that of *wu wei*, normally translated as "actionless action" or "non-coercive action." Too often it is mistranslated as "non-action," which really misses the point and leads people to mistake Taoism for a sort of world-rejecting Nihilism[8]. The practitioner of *wu wei* goes about his or her daily life just as anyone else. The difference is that he or she does not struggle nor contend with obstacles or adversaries. Rather, like water, the *wu wei* approach will patiently find a way around an impediment or patiently wear it down rather than confront it head on. Taoism implies that it is an enormous waste of energy to attack anything, and that to do so usually results in a life-denying injury, retribution or disaster somewhere down the line. Such an approach, of course, can only be effectively taken on board when one has first developed a profound patience and humility in their personality.

Humility

Every philosophical system worth its salt advocates the practice of humility yet few of them explain precisely why it's important. The Golden Rule comes close (treat others as you would have them treat you), but even this relies on a heavy dose of top-down moralizing, i.e. "because it's the right thing to do." Taoism, on the other hand, takes a more explicitly organic, systems theory[9] approach. Namely, since a group is stronger than an individual, making yourself attractive and indispensable to others is prone to solidify your inclusion and trust within that group as well as increase access to its resources.

This mirrors the principle of investing—a little sacrifice now will result in a much greater payoff later. So, by strengthening the invisible bonds of loyalty and cooperation, feedback loops can be created in human and societal relationships that not only increase the sum total of virtue but also help to suppress selfish and misanthropic behavior in others. Just as investment in a decaying city center can have extreme run-on effects to its citizens and outliers, in the long run, so can humble and generous investment in one's relationships or groups improve the

---

[8] Buddhism has famously suffered the same misrepresentation.

[9] Systems theory is a relatively new scientific approach which aims to dissect the mechanics and dynamics of natural systems. It is arguably the closest that Western science comes to Taoism. Most of the ideas in the *Tao Te Ching* are supported by similar notions found in this fledgling field of study.

quality of life for all concerned, with ripple effects expanding ever-outwards.

Ironically, the practitioner of humility is likely to be trusted with greater power and influence. Though seemingly contradictory, this is a phenomenon alluded to again and again in the *Tao Te Ching*: That those who subsume themselves in a group or relationship for the benefit of others are ultimately rewarded with greater resources. Conversely, those who pursue power for its own sake are doomed to fail—robust systems will ultimately reject a selfish agent as a form of cancer. This is how biological systems survive: by reflexively destroying or sacrificing cancerous agents that threaten to sabotage the overall arrangement. This "immune system" applies to human social systems, and, in case of the well-trained mind, psychological ones as well.

Compassion

The notion that nature is compassionate is one which most scientists would take immediate issue with. In fact the *Tao Te Ching* itself says "nature is impartial," that it looks upon people no different than it looks upon refuse. And yet one of the most iconic verses (67) claims that compassion is at the base of the Tao and that all things proceed from compassion. So what's going on here?

The compassion championed by the *Tao Te Ching* is something more akin to interconnectedness and cooperation—that is, the realization that everything is connected to and reliant on everything else in a grand, mutually-reinforcing ecosystem. Therefore, when chapter 5 says it looks upon man no different than it does trash, this does not necessarily intend to belittle mankind, but possibly to reassess what may appear to be rubbish.

At several points throughout the book, we are recommended to consider those who seem to be outsiders or ignored or disenfranchised and to recognize that despite initial appearances, they may have much to offer, and that to reject parts of the ecosystem is to needlessly impoverish it. To be compassionate to the less-fortunate not only helps raise them up, but ourselves, and our entire society as well.

Moderation

Though our world religions differ on all sorts of topics, one they almost universally agree on is the dangerousness of desire.

As with humility, it's rarely spelled out exactly why desire is dangerous, only that we should avoid it. With only basic admonitions like "don't covet the things of your neighbor" (Judeo-Christian) and "desire is the root of all suffering" (Buddhism), we are meant to infer that desire is prone to be punished by some mysterious force in the universe (deities or karma). However, if we could make sense of desire and its logical consequences, we might better defend against its dangers. When decoded, the *Tao Te Ching* neatly illuminates the issue.

One of the problems in defending ourselves against the ravages of desire is defining it in the first place. Isn't desire a big part of who we are? If we didn't give in to our desires for food and drink and shelter we'd all be dead in a week. To a lesser degree, the same goes for human interaction, affection, mental stimulation, basic freedom and all sort of other primal human wants, without which we tend to suffer. And what of grand plans like building a skyscraper or writing a symphony? Are these not propelled by human desire? Are they really so bad? Should we all still be living in mud huts and drumming on rocks?[10]

As we've explained when discussing *wu wei*, the Taoist is not against action for action's sake. Creative and fortifying pursuits, after all, are a part of the great unfolding of humanity within the greater sphere of Tao. However, the practitioner of *wu wei* allows things to unfold at its natural pace, to let the pieces of a plan naturally fall together.

Desire is very different from this. It impels one to grasp at goals and rewards immediately, without consideration or patience. Thus one who desires tends to upset the harmoniousness of systems which are a part of him (biological, psychological) and of which he is a part (societal, environmental). When confronted with desire, an accomplished Taoist will calmly redirect those impulses so that they don't cause any harm to themselves, others, or systems as a whole. Rather than immediately rush in to fill a void, the Taoist first takes stock of the empty space and maps out its dimensions. In this way, targets of opportunity can be slowly redirected or sublimated in accordance with the big picture rather than

---

[10] Though there are many arguments which suggest that we were happier when we were living in mud huts and drumming on rocks, this is beside the point. Creativity and grand human endeavor is not necessarily anathema to the Tao, and in many ways can be seen as a great extension of its creative power. The difficulties and challenges that civilization presents are better overcome by adhering to Taoist principles rather than yearning for the lost golden age which Lao Tzu suggests existed prior to civilization.

the short-term satisfying of immediate and self-serving needs. This of course requires considerable practice and patience.

Patience

Through the inculcation of a profound patience, Taoism introduces informed choice into every equation, allowing the raw energy of base impulsivity to be employed from a more pragmatic perspective. As dispassionate as it may sound, this is the essential difference between the great engineer and the merely energetic. Modern culture may labor under a mythology that romanticizes and elevates the impulsive, but most great accomplishments in history have been the result of enduring immersion and affectionate engagement, rather than dramatic and reckless stabs in the dark.[11] The reason for this is simple, and yet hardly ever spelled out: because our world is so much larger than we are. It takes considerable time and attention to incorporate and make sense of its bigger-picture patterns.

Of course, it goes without saying that the virtue of patience extends to more aspects of the human condition than just our so-called "great accomplishments"—patience in relationships, career, investing, and diet usually trump quick-and-easy schemes in the long run. Given our universal struggles in all these fields, it seems that patience is one of the hardest traits for humans to develop. Moreover, the pace and pressure of modern life appears to thwart that development at every turn.

Sadly, there's little solace to be found in knowing that this was also such a problem in Lao Tzu's time, 2500 years ago. Is this something rather hard-wired within us? Or a pernicious side effect of civilized lifestyles? It seems likely that each have their influence.

Flexibility

One of the most renowned metaphors in the *Tao Te Ching* is the comparison between mentally flexible people and green plants. Green plants tend to bend with impact instead of breaking, and bounce back when the pressure is relieved. Conversely, dry and inflexible ones will break, often beyond repair. Moreover, flexible plants will grow and find their way around obstacles and into fresh design space, while the inflexible will remain immobile and stick more deeply in their rut.

---

[11] This brings to mind Edison's famous quote: "Genius is 1 percent inspiration and 99 percent perspiration." Only, for the Taoist sage, the perspiration is meant to be the most rewarding part.

Accordingly, it follows that to be flexible is to be full of life, while to be stiff and brittle is to be old and unmoving. These principles are obvious when we evaluate concrete objects, but they're potentially just as appropriate when we assess the way people act, feel and cooperate with others in their lives.

Since bullheadedness is admired by many in our modern culture, flexibility is often mistaken for weakness. "No compromises!" may be the slogan of idealists everywhere, yet professional negotiators know that intractability is the kiss of death. Instead, they collect strategies and tools which can locate and loosen the soft veins of gold in even the most hardened adversary. In doing this, they are able to engineer solutions that benefit all, and thus do the sacred, eternal work of evolution: fashioning synthesis from apparent antithesis[12].

Like a master negotiator, a Taoist sage is one who knows how to capitalize upon with the natural flow of things. Note that the word "negotiation," also applies to the negotiation of a river, by mapping out and aligning with its flow.

Self-awareness

It's all well and good to make a list of principles and instruct someone to follow them. But humans are saddled with diverging drives which often make it hard to initiate and maintain a course. As Lao Tzu puts it in chapter 53:

> *If we had the tiniest bit of sense,*
> *We would stay on the thoroughfare of Tao,*
> *Avoiding ill-fated off-ramps.*
> *The high road is broad and smooth,*
> *Yet for some strange reason,*
> *People are prone to veer into dangerous detours.*

To keep us on the so-called "high road," religions all over the world have all prescribed a similar type of meditative practice meant to put us

---

[12] Though often mistakenly attributed to Hegel, the notion of thesis-antithesis-synthesis was actually a theory of Johann Fichte which aimed to describe how change comes about in intellectual systems. Also called the dialectical method, it seems to mirror the worldview put forth in the Tao Te Ching—that the generalized poles of yin and yang give rise to novelty via their interpenetrative tension and flow.

in greater control of our actions, drives, and thoughts. It's as if we're frantically running through a maze, trying to find the correct path, and expecting it will be revealed via increasing our level of frenzy. Rather, by intentionally stopping for a moment and quieting down we can let the natural patterns both within us and without us present themselves. Meditation can be seen as a sort of wu wei of the mind, in which by doing nothing, great accomplishments are set in motion.

Although the image of the holy sage seated in meditation can be seen as a sort of "retreat" from the world, from the Taoist point of view, precisely the opposite is true: Meditation is a tool to help promote the flourishing of life. It is only because humans are burdened with brains that are powerful but ill-adapted to our complex modern world that we require this regular "tuning" to help us align ourselves with it properly. Ultimately, this regular tuning can help us operate in harmony with society, biology, ecology and all other natural systems. Without it, we are in danger of working at cross purposes with the world, to the detriment of both.

Vitality

All religions change over time, normally starting as more of a philosophical movement and then ultimately becoming heavily politicized and laden with superstition. Some notable thinkers and movements[13] have argued that all the Axial Age religions have the same basic messages and ideas but have only diverged as a result of time and outside interests. Taoism is certainly no different in this respect.

There is some disagreement about this in academic circles, but it seems that the original "philosophical" Taoism of Lao Tzu broke off into a schism and the new branch became embroidered with gods and superstitions and health rituals. This newer version is commonly referred to as "religious" Taoism. In this more ornate form of Taoism, blended as it with Chinese folk traditions, there is a great focus on techniques for achieving immortality through the balancing of yin yang in the body

---

[13] Aldous Huxley helped re-popularize this notion in his book *The Perennial Philosophy*. Unitarian Universalism is an organized religion which seeks to find generic common ground in all religions. Yet it is perhaps the broader New Age publishing world which has done the most to advocate the idea that all spiritual traditions stem from the same source. However, it often relies more upon creative imagination than hard scholarship in doing so.

through traditional medicine and the cultivation of a mysterious life energy known as "chi."

Though this introduction and translation of the *Tao Te Ching* you hold here takes the perspective of the original philosophical branch of Taoism, the notion of extending vitality is still just as important. Only, rather than using herbs and exercises to increase lifespan and health, a much more basic and broader approach is undertaken.

Rather than merely prescribing specific life enhancement techniques, it could be said that life enhancement is at the very essence of the book itself. In other words, the aim of the *Tao Te Ching* and Taoism is to enhance vitality in every sense of the word, in all living systems, everywhere. The way to do this is not necessarily via specific medicines or exercises, but by understanding and developing these very principles listed here—conditions and approaches under which all living systems tend to flourish.

After all, there is a reason the *Tao Te Ching* has been translated so many times—it is not just a book about life, it is a book that *is itself alive*. Since it was designed to follow its own principles, it is ever-renewed and adapted to a changing world by the successive generations which shuffle along its prescribed path.

In other words, as we walk upon the way, we also contribute to its creation.

Happy travels!

Additional Notes

If you would like to be ordained for free as a Jedi minister you can do so at The Ministry of Jediism: www.ism.co/jediism. It's fast, free and easy.

The original *Tao Te Ching* upon which *The Tao of the Jedi* is based is available for download as a free ebook at www.ism.co/library/daoism. There is also a link on that page to a longer, annotated version available for purchase at Amazon.com which contains essays explaining each verse.

Male pronouns are often used in this book to signify human beings in general, rather than resorting to awkward grammatical constructions like "he or she." No masculine bias is intended. The anonymous people alluded to could be either female or male.

If you'd like to discuss this book with the author and others, please visit www.ism.co/forums/jediism. Corrections, suggestions, additions and criticisms are most welcome!